Twenty to Make

Sugar Dogs

Frances McNaughton

Search Press

First published in Great Britain 2014

Search Press Limited
Wellwood, North Farm Road,
Tunbridge Wells, Kent TN2 3DR

Text copyright © Frances McNaughton 2014

Photographs by Paul Bricknell at
Search Press Studios

Photographs and design copyright
© Search Press Ltd 2014

Print ISBN: 978-1-84448-966-4
EPUB ISBN: 978-1-78126-190-3
Mobi ISBN: 978-1-78126-191-0

Suppliers
If you have difficulty in obtaining any of the
materials and equipment mentioned in this book,
then please visit the Search Press website for
details of suppliers: www.searchpress.com

Printed in China

Contents

Introduction

Dogs touch many of our lives and, although I don't have one myself, I have been lucky to meet some very sweet dogs over the years. When choosing which models to make for this book, some of those dogs were the obvious choices for me to include.

As in my other books, I have included edible sugar candy sticks as supports for some of the dogs, which means that they are completely edible. These sticks can easily be made in advance, as they dry hard and can be stored until needed. Some sweet shops sell them too, so that can save time.

Following my other books in the 'Twenty to make' range, I have tried to keep the basic shapes simple, using readily available sugar modelling paste, and keeping the modelling tools to a minimum.

Beginners will have fun creating these models and, with a little experience, will be able to make different breeds and colours of dog by adapting shapes and positions. More advanced sugarcrafters may find further inspiration within these pages to produce models of their own pets.

Although I have used sugar modelling paste and sugarpaste (also known as fondant icing or rolled fondant), these cute dogs could also be made in marzipan, chocolate modelling paste or non-edible clays.

Materials and tools

Materials

Modelling paste is used for the main parts of the dogs. It can be made by kneading one teaspoon (5ml) of CMC/Tylose into 500g (1lb) of commercial sugarpaste (also known as fondant icing or rolled fondant).

Sugarpaste (also known as fondant icing or rolled fondant) works well for making long fur and fluff. It can be blended and textured as it stays soft longer than modelling paste.

Clear piping gel This can be used to brighten eyes or to stick on fur if dampening with water does not work.

Strong gel paste colours are used for mixing in to white modelling paste to make solid colours. Colours used in the book are: blue, purple, black, dark brown, chestnut, red and green.

Black and pale pink food colour pens Used to add detail to dogs.

Edible candy sticks These are used to support dogs and as necks or legs. They can be made easily in advance by rolling sugar modelling paste into short stick shapes and leaving them to dry until hard. They are often available commercially in sweet shops.

Small black edible sugar pearls These make good eyes and noses.

Black and brown edible powder food colour Used to colour dogs.

Food grade alcohol This is used mixed with edible powder food colour, for painting.

Modelling paste and sugarpaste (fondant icing or rolled fondant).

Tools

Small sharp pointed scissors These can be used for cutting paste and snipping details.

Tea strainer/small sieve This is used for making fur and fluff.

Silicone multi-mould This is used in some projects to make the tiny bow.

Small circle, petal and oval cutters These are used to make parts of the dogs such as ears.

Dusting brush This is used to apply edible powder food colours.

Small scales These small, accurate scales are good for weighing out modelling paste and sugarpaste.

Stitching wheel This is used to add a stitched effect.

Plastic food bag/airtight box For keeping paste soft.

Cutting wheel This can be used for cutting out shapes.

Dogbone tool/small ball tool Used for modelling.

Petal veining tool This is used to create a fluted edge.

Dresden tool This is used to make indents for eyes and noses, and for creating texture.

Fine paintbrushes Used for painting on food colour.

Water brush This is used to dampen modelling paste ready for sticking.

Small, non-stick rolling pin Used to roll out modelling paste.

Thin palette knife Used in all the projects for loosening the models from the work surface, and for creating texture or marks.

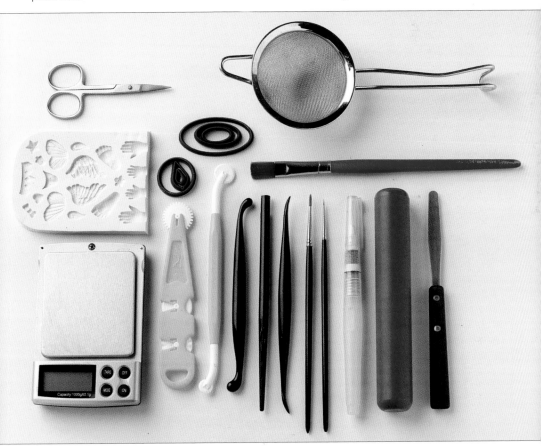

7

Labrador Puppy

Materials:

25g (just under 1oz) cream-
   coloured modelling paste

Edible candy stick

Edible black sugar pearls

Dark brown edible powder
   food colour

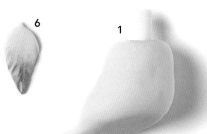

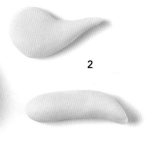

Tools:

Small petal cutter

Dresden tool

Dusting brush

Water brush

Small, non-stick rolling pin

Thin palette knife

Instructions:

1 Shape 10g ($^1/_3$oz) of modelling paste to a 3cm (1¼in) oval for the body. Insert a candy stick right through, as a support. Cut the stick to form a short neck. Pinch and shape a small pointed tail. Stand the body up.

2 Cut 6g ($^1/_5$oz) of modelling paste into four equal pieces for the legs. Roll each leg to about 3cm (1¼in). For the back legs, flatten the top end. Mark toes with the palette knife. Attach the legs to the body by dampening with a little water.

3 For the head, make a 5g ($^1/_6$oz) ball of modelling paste. Roll one end with your fingers to form the muzzle. Mark the eyes and nose with a Dresden tool. Push the black sugar pearls in for the eyes and nose.

4 Dampen the candy stick neck, and gently push the head into place on the body.

5 Make two very tiny sausages of paste and attach over the eyes.

6 Roll out a small amount of paste thinly and cut out two ears using the small petal cutter as shown. Mark the surface with the Dresden tool, then brush the surface gently with dark brown powder food colour. Dampen the underneath surface of the ears with the water brush and attach the ears at the back of the head, folding them forwards towards the face.

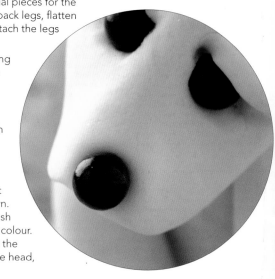

Dachshund

Materials:

20g (²/₃oz) chestnut
  modelling paste
Edible candy stick
Edible black sugar pearls

Tools:

2cm (¾in) oval cutter
Dresden tool
Water brush
Thin palette knife
Small, non-stick rolling pin

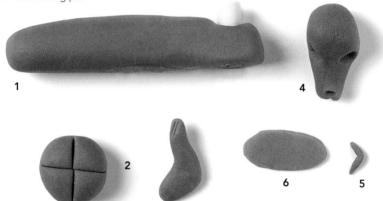

Instructions:

1 Shape 10g (¹/₃oz) of paste to a 6cm (2³/₈in) sausage for the body. Push a short candy stick vertically through the sausage at the neck end. Make a tiny short pointed cone for the tail and stick it on.

2 Cut 2g (¹/₁₂oz) of paste into four equal pieces for the legs. Roll each to form a 2cm (¾in) sausage. Curve each leg and mark toes with a knife.

3 Attach the legs to the sides of the body with all the toe ends pointing forwards.

4 Shape 2.5g (¹/₁₀oz) paste to a long pear shape. Shape the fat end of the head to form a higher forehead. Mark the eyes and nose with a Dresden tool. Insert edible black sugar pearls for the eyes and nose. Mark the mouth using a knife.

5 Make two very tiny sausages of paste and attach over the eyes.

6 Roll out the paste thinly and cut out two small oval shapes for ears. Attach them to the top of the head facing backwards, and then fold them over to look floppy, as shown.

Schnauzer

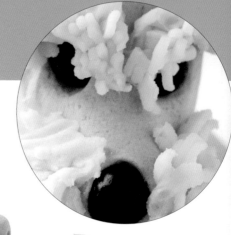

Materials:

30g (1oz) green modelling paste

Edible sugar candy sticks painted grey with black food colour

15g (½oz) grey modelling paste

Small amount of pale grey sugarpaste for fluff

Edible black sugar pearls

Clear piping gel (optional)

Tools:

Small petal cutter

Dresden tool

Water brush

Thin palette knife

Tea strainer/small sieve

Instructions:

1 Shape the green paste to a 6cm (2³/₈in) oval for the base and texture the surface to look like grass using the Dresden tool. Push in two 3cm (1¼in) candy sticks at an angle as shown, then two vertically, with 3cm (1¼in) between the front and back pairs to allow space for the body to stick on. Trim the tops of the vertical legs to be level with the top of the back legs.

2 Shape 10g (¹/₃oz) of grey paste to a 3cm (1¼in) cone for the body. Pinch and shape a small vertical tail at the narrow end. Push in an edible candy stick vertically for the neck. Dampen the tops of the legs and push the body into place, head end above the vertical legs.

3 Shape 2.5g (¹/₁₀₀oz) of grey paste to a long pear shape. Turn up the narrow end slightly for the nose. Pinch and shape the sides of the muzzle to make them hang down more. Shape the fat end of the head gently to form a higher forehead. Mark the eyes and nose with a Dresden tool and insert edible black sugar pearls. Dampen the top of the neck and press the head into place.

4 Roll out the paste thinly and cut out two small petal shapes for the ears. Attach them to the back of the head with the points upwards, and then fold them over and form them to look angled, as shown.

5 Dampen the areas at the base of the legs, cheeks, and eyebrows where the fluff will go. Push grey sugarpaste through a tea strainer/small sieve to make fluff. When it is the length you want, cut it off with a knife and attach it to the dampened areas on the dog. Press into place with the Dresden tool as using your fingers would flatten the fluff. If you have trouble getting it to stay on, use clear piping gel as a glue instead of dampening with water.

Scotty Dog

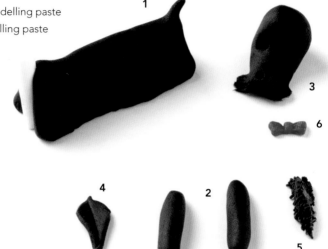

Materials:

25g (just under 1oz) black modelling paste
Very small piece of red modelling paste
Edible candy stick
Edible black sugar pearls
Clear piping gel (optional)

Tools:

Small petal cutter
Dresden tool
Dusting brush
Water brush
Thin palette knife
Tea strainer/small sieve
Multi-mould (tiny bow)
Small non-stick rolling pin

Instructions:

1 Shape 15g (½oz) of black paste to a 5cm (2in) sausage for the body. Flatten the sides to form a long triangle. Pinch and shape a small tail. Mark long fur with the Dresden tool. Attach an edible candy stick at the front end for the neck.

2 Shape two small pea-sized pieces of black paste to sausages the same height as the body. Dampen and press them into place to hide the candy stick support. Mark long fur with the Dresden tool.

3 Shape 2.5g (¹/₁₀oz) paste to a long pear shape for the head. Turn up the narrow end slightly for the nose. Pinch and shape the sides of the muzzle to make them hang down more. Use the Dresden tool to texture the muzzle. Shape the fat end of the head gently to form a higher forehead. Mark the eyes and nose with a Dresden tool and insert edible black sugar pearls. Dampen the top of the neck and press the head into place.

4 Roll out the paste thinly and cut out two small petal shapes for the ears. Attach them to the back of the head with the points upwards.

5 Dampen the eyebrows where the fluff will go. Push black paste through the tea strainer or sieve to make fluff. When you have the length you want, cut it off with a knife and attach it to form the eyebrows. Press into place with a Dresden tool as your fingers may flatten the fluff. If you have trouble getting it to stay on, use clear piping gel as a glue instead of dampening with water.

6 Make a tiny bow by pressing red modelling paste into the tiny bow mould. Dampen and attach to the neck.

Yorkshire Terrier

Materials:

15g (½oz) cream-coloured modelling paste

10g (⅓oz) chestnut modelling paste

Edible candy stick

Edible black sugar pearls

Brown and grey edible powder food colour

Tools:

Small petal cutter

Dresden tool

Dusting brush

Water brush

Thin palette knife

Plastic food bag/airtight box

Small non-stick rolling pin

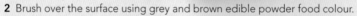

Instructions:

1 Shape 15g (½oz) of cream paste into a ball for the body. Insert a dampened edible candy stick, and model to a flat-bottomed 4cm (1½in) cone as shown. Pinch and shape a tail at the base, and mark an indentation for the front legs using the Dresden tool. Texture with the same tool to create long fur. Thin the edge of the tail to look like fur.

2 Brush over the surface using grey and brown edible powder food colour.

3 Shape 5g (⅙oz) of paste to a short pear shape for the head. Turn up the narrow end slightly for the nose. Shape the fat end gently to form a higher forehead. Mark the eyes and nose with a Dresden tool. Insert edible black sugar pearls for the eyes and nose. Dampen the top of the neck and press the head into place, tilting backwards to look cute. For best results, leave the dog to dry overnight before adding the fur.

4 Shape lots of tiny 1–2cm (⅜–¾in) sausages of chestnut paste and keep them soft under plastic. Start placing them in the middle of the head and nose, so that the fur hangs down. Mark with a knife or Dresden tool to look like fur. Make sure that the eyes and nose can be seen.

5 Roll out chestnut paste thinly and cut out petals for ears. Mark lines for the fur. Attach to the back of the head, points upwards.

Pug

Materials:

40g (1⅓oz) cream-coloured
   modelling paste

Edible candy stick

Edible black sugar pearls

Dark brown and black edible
   powder food colour

Food grade alcohol for
   painting

Clear piping gel

Black food colour pen

Tools:

Small petal cutter

Small, non-stick
   rolling pin

Dresden tool

Fine paintbrush

Dusting brush

Water brush

Thin palette knife

4

1

7

6

2

3

5

Instructions:

1 Shape 20g (⅔oz) of
modelling paste to a 4cm
(1½in) oval for the body
and insert a candy stick right
through, as a support. Cut the
stick to form a short neck.
Stand the body up.

2 Make a tiny pointed
cone of paste for the tail. Curl
it up and attach the fat end under the body.

3 Cut an 8g (¼oz) piece of modelling paste into four pieces for the
legs. Roll each leg to about 4cm (1½in). For the back legs, flatten the
top end. Mark toes with the palette knife. Attach the legs to
the body in the position shown by dampening with a little water.
Draw paw pads on the base of the back feet using the black food
colour pen.

4 Make a 10g (⅓oz) ball of paste for the head and roll one end to
narrow it slightly. Pinch the narrow end down on each side to form
the muzzle. Mark holes for the eyes and nose using the Dresden
tool. Insert black sugar pearls for the eyes. Shape a small pea-sized
piece of paste to a teardrop shape for the lower jaw and attach it
to the head, with the rounded end just under the nose to make the
mouth. Dampen the candy-stick neck and attach the head.

5 For the wrinkled folds of the neck, shape a pea-sized piece of paste to form a 4cm (1⅝in) sausage. Flatten it slightly and mark wrinkles lengthways with the Dresden tool. Dampen and attach it around the neck, joining it at the back and pressing it into place with the Dresden tool. Allow to dry for a couple of hours or overnight.

6 Roll out the paste thinly and cut out two small petal shapes for ears. Attach them to the back of the head with the points upwards, and then fold them over as shown.

7 For the wrinkly face, make three or four thin sausages of paste approximately 5cm (2in) long. Dampen the face. Attach one or two between the nose and the eyes, shaping to form the jowls. Press in the edible black sugar pearl for the nose. Then add more sausages of paste above the eyes, shaping to form the wrinkles. It can help to form more wrinkles by pressing in with the Dresden tool while shaping them. Make sure the eyes can be seen.

8 Use dark brown powder food colour to brush over the wrinkles above the eyes and the feet, tail, ears and face.

9 Paint the front of the face and tips of the ears with black food colouring mixed with alcohol.

10 Squeeze two blobs of clear piping gel in to give a shine to the eyes.

Great Dane

Materials:

50g (1¾oz) red modelling paste

30g (1oz) cream-coloured modelling paste

Small amount of pink modelling paste

Edible black sugar pearl

Dark brown edible powder food colour

Food grade alcohol for painting

Black food colour pen

Tools:

Small, non-stick rolling pin

Small petal cutter

Dresden tool

Fine paintbrush

Dusting brush

Water brush

Thin palette knife

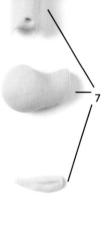

Instructions:

1 Shape the red modelling paste to form a pillow by pinching the corners and flattening it.

2 Shape 10g (⅓oz) of the cream modelling paste to a 6cm (2⅜in) curved cone for the body. Flatten slightly.

3 Cut a 10g (⅓oz) piece of paste into four pieces for the legs. Form each one into a 6cm (2⅜in) long carrot shape. Shape to form the joints.

4 Lay one front leg and one back leg on the pillow; lay the body on top, with the wide end for the chest. Gently lift and dampen underneath when you have the position you like.

5 Dampen and attach the other legs.

6 Shape a small thin carrot for the tail and attach it to the body.

7 Make a 5g (⅙oz) long pear shape for the head (and top jaw). Pinch the paste down at the sides to form the muzzle. Mark the sleeping eyes with a knife. Insert the edible black pearl for the nose. Make a tiny pink flattened cone for the tongue. Attach it to the top jaw as shown. Make another small cone of cream-coloured paste for the bottom jaw, and stick that in place under the tongue. Dampen and attach the head to the body and cushion.

8 Roll out the paste thinly and cut out two small petal shapes for ears. Attach them to the sides of the head with the points upwards, and then fold them over as shown.

9 Use dark brown edible powder food colour to brush over the paws, tail, ears and face.

10 Paint the front of the face, the eyes and the tips of the ears with dark brown edible powder food colour mixed with alcohol.

11 Draw pads on the base of the paws using the black food colour pen.

Alsatian

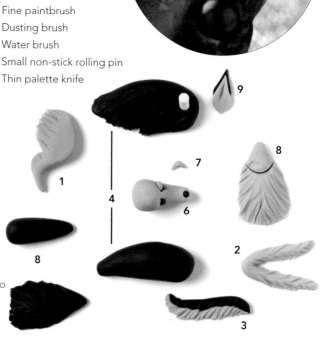

Materials:

25g (just under 1oz) tan modelling paste

20g (²/₃oz) black modelling paste

Edible candy stick

Edible black sugar pearls

Dark brown and black edible powder food colour

Food grade alcohol for painting

Black food colour pen

Tools:

Small petal cutter

Dresden tool

Fine paintbrush

Dusting brush

Water brush

Small non-stick rolling pin

Thin palette knife

Instructions:

1 Shape 5g (¹/₆oz) of the tan paste to a 5cm (2in) carrot for a back leg. Flatten the wide end. Bend and pinch to form a 'Z' shape for the joints. Use a Dresden tool to drag the back edge of the leg as shown to make the long fur effect. Draw pads on the base of the paw using the black food colour pen. Make two.

2 For the front legs, make 2.5g (¹/₁₀oz) of the tan paste into an 8cm (3¹/₈in) sausage shape. Bend in the middle to make a 'V' shape. Mark the fur with the Dresden tool as shown.

3 For the tail, shape a small pea-sized piece of black paste to a 5cm (2in) sausage and repeat with a tan piece. Press together lengthways. Flatten the tan edge slightly and drag the paste with the Dresden tool to form long fur. Curve the tail a little.

4 Shape 15g (½oz) of black paste to a 4cm (1½in) cone for the body. Flatten slightly down one edge. Drag the paste with the Dresden tool to form long fur. Push a short 3cm (1¼in) candy stick vertically into the wide end to support the head.

5 Put the body and legs together, dampening each piece to stick. Place one back leg on the surface; attach the tail at the top of the leg; lay the body over the top, then lay the other back leg over the back of the body in the position shown. Raise the front end of the body and attach the front legs underneath.

6 Shape 10g (¹/₃oz) of tan paste to a 4cm (1½in) pear shape. Pinch and shape the narrow end to form the muzzle. Shape the wide end to form a high forehead. Make indentations for the eyes and nose, and insert the edible black sugar pearls. Dampen the candy stick neck, and attach the head. Leave to dry for a couple of hours or overnight.

7 Make two very tiny sausages of tan paste for the eyebrows; bend each to form an angle. Dampen over the eyes and attach the eyebrows.

8 Chest and shoulders. Shape 5g ($^1/_6$oz) each of black and tan paste to 4cm (1½in) long cone shapes. Flatten each around the edges with your fingers. Feather the edges with the Dresden tool to look like fur. Attach the narrow end of the black one from the back of the head to drape over the shoulders and blend in with the Dresden tool. Cut a curve into the narrow end of the tan piece; dampen the back of it and attach under the chin to drape over the tops of the legs. Blend in with the Dresden tool.

9 Roll out both pastes thinly and cut out two small petal shapes in each colour for the ears. Lay each tan piece on top of the black, so that the black still shows. Mark down the centre of each with the Dresden tool. Attach to the back of the head with the points upwards.

10 Paint the black detail on the face using black powder food colour mixed with alcohol. Also paint edges to blend between black and tan parts of the body.

11 Brush black powder food colour over paws and face to soften edges.

12 Draw pads on the base of the back paws using the black food colour pen.

Border Terrier

Materials:

20g (²/₃oz) cream-coloured
  modelling paste

Edible candy stick

Edible black sugar pearls

Dark brown powder food colour

Tools:

Small petal cutter

Dresden tool

Dusting brush

Water brush

Thin palette knife

Instructions:

1 When making each part of this little dog, it is easiest if you texture and mark the fur with a Dresden tool and knife before you attach it to the next piece.

2 Shape 10g (¹/₃oz) of paste to a 4cm (1½in) sausage, then pinch and roll one end to form a short pointed tail. Push in a short candy stick at an angle at the neck end and texture as in step 1.

3 Cut 5g (¹/₆oz) of paste into four for the legs. Shape them into 3cm (1¼in) carrots, flatten the fat end and curve it towards the paw, as shown. Texture as in step 1.

4 Lay the back legs flat on the surface, paws ponting outwards. Lay the back of the body over them, and dampen to stick them in place. Draw pads on the base of the back paws using the black food colour pen.

5 Attach the front legs to the sides at the chest end, so that the paws point forwards.

6 Shape 2.5g (¹/₁₀oz) paste to a short pear shape for the head. Turn up the narrow end slightly for the nose. Press under the nose with the Dresden tool for the top of the mouth. Shape the fat end of the head to gently form a higher forehead. Mark the eyes and nose with a Dresden tool and insert edible black sugar pearls. Shape a tiny carrot of paste for the bottom jaw and stick it into place with the rounded end forming the front of the mouth. Texture as before.

24

7 Dampen the candy stick neck and attach the head. Tilt it at a cute angle.

8 Make two very tiny sausages of paste and attach over the eyes.

9 Roll out the paste thinly and cut out two small petal shapes for ears. Texture with the Dresden tool. Attach them to the back of the head with the points upwards, and then fold them over as shown.

10 Brush the whole dog gently with dark brown powder food colour.

Bulldog Puppy

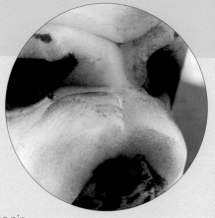

Materials:

40g (1¹/₃oz) white modelling paste

50g (1¾oz) brown modelling paste

Edible candy stick

Edible black sugar pearls

Brown and black edible powder food colour

Food grade alcohol for painting

Clear piping gel

Tools:

Dresden tool

Dogbone tool/ small ball tool

Fine paintbrush

Dusting brush

Water brush

Thin palette knife

Small non-stick rolling pin

Instructions:

1 Make two 5cm (2in) sausages of white paste for the legs using 5g (¹/₆oz) each. Curve the legs to a 'C' shape. Pinch the paws forward. Leave to dry overnight over a dowel or paintbrush handle.

2 Roll out brown paste thickly for the doormat and cut to 8 x 6cm (3¹/₈ x 2³/₈in). Texture the top with the Dresden tool and mark the sides with a knife to create the look of a fringe.

3 Shape 20g (²/₃oz) of white paste to a 5cm (2in) cone shape for the body. Mark two indentations across

it where the legs will go. Turn it over and push in a short candy stick to support the head at the fat end. Dampen the hardened legs and attach them under the body. Make sure that the toes are pointing to the fat end. Dampen under the paws and stick them to the doormat, pushing in slightly. For best results leave to dry for a couple of hours or overnight.

4 Shape 10g (¹/₃oz) of white paste to a short pear shape for the head. Pinch down the sides of the narrow end to form the muzzle. Mark indentations to the eyes and nose. Insert edible black sugar pearls. Shape a tiny cone for the bottom jaw. Stick in place with the rounded end under the nose. Shape two tiny balls for the ears. Dampen and attach them to the head. Support the back of the ear with a finger and push a dogbone tool/small ball tool in to form the cupped ear. Dampen the neck and push the head on to the body.

5 For the wrinkly neck, shape a pea-sized piece of white paste to form a 5cm (2in) sausage, flatten it slightly and mark wrinkles lengthwise with the Dresden tool. Dampen and attach it around the neck, joining it at the back and pressing it into place with the Dresden tool. Repeat, adding more sausages and wrinkles down the back.

6 For the wrinkly face, make five or six thin sausages of paste approximately 5cm (2in) long. Dampen the face. Attach two or three over the nose, shaping to form the jowls. Then add more above the eyes, shaping to form the wrinkles. It can help to press in with the Dresden tool while shaping them. Make sure the eyes can be seen.

7 Paint patches on the body and face with brown and black edible powder food colour mixed with alcohol. Brush the muzzle and around the eyes with black powder food colour.

8 Make a tiny pointed cone of paste for the tail. Curl it up and attach the fat end to the body.

Bichon Frise

Materials:

20g (²/₃oz) white modelling paste
20g (²/₃oz) white sugarpaste
50g (1¾oz) red modelling paste
Edible candy stick
Edible black sugar pearls
Black food colour pen

Tools:

Small non-stick rolling pin
Petal veining tool
Small petal shape cutter
Dresden tool
Dusting brush
Water brush
Thin palette knife
Tea strainer/small sieve

Instructions:

1 Roll out red paste thinly. Cut a blanket
8 x 6cm (3¹/₈ x 2³/₈in). Frill the edge by
rolling with a petal veining tool.

2 Shape 5g (¹/₆oz) of white modelling paste to a 4cm (1½in)
cone for the body. Push in a short candy stick at the fat end for
the neck as shown.

3 Shape 2.5g (¹/₁₀oz) of white modelling paste to a short pear
shape for the head. Turn up the narrow end slightly for the nose.
Shape the fat end gently to form a higher forehead. Mark the eyes
and nose with a Dresden tool and insert edible black sugar pearls.
Dampen the top of the neck and press the head into place.

4 Cut a 5g (¹/₆oz) piece of paste into four equal pieces for the legs.
Roll each to form a 3cm (1¼in) sausage. Bend the front legs to form
an 'L' shape and attach to the top of the body with the paws pointing
away from the head. Attach the back legs, bent in the same way, to
the side of the body at the tail end, paws pointing to the head. Draw
pads on the base of the back paws using the black food colour pen.

5 Lay the dog on the blanket.

6 Dampen the whole dog, (except the feet on the back legs) where the fluff will go. Push the white sugarpaste through the tea strainer/small sieve to make fluff. When you have the length you want, cut it off with a knife and attach it to the dampened areas on the dog. Press into place with Dresden tool as your fingers may flatten the fluff. If you have trouble getting it to stay on, use piping gel as a glue instead of dampening with water. Make the ears and tail from the fluff, and stick it directly to the blanket. Make sure that the eyes and nose are visible.

Bassett Hound

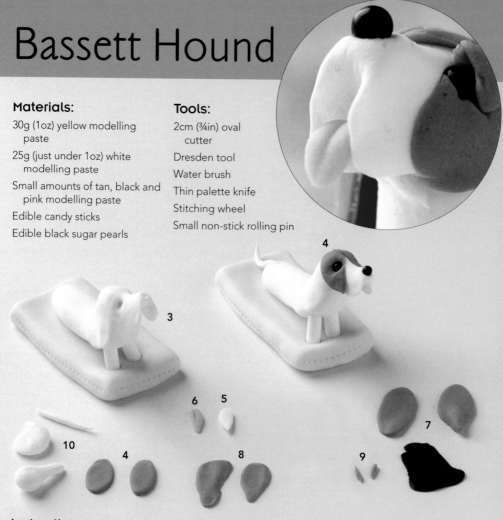

Materials:

30g (1oz) yellow modelling paste

25g (just under 1oz) white modelling paste

Small amounts of tan, black and pink modelling paste

Edible candy sticks

Edible black sugar pearls

Tools:

2cm (¾in) oval cutter

Dresden tool

Water brush

Thin palette knife

Stitching wheel

Small non-stick rolling pin

Instructions:

1 Shape the yellow modelling paste into a pillow a 8 x 3cm (3⅛ x 1¼in). Mark around the edge with the stitching wheel. At one end, push in two 2cm (¾in) edible candy sticks vertically, close together for the dog's front legs.

2 Shape 15g (½oz) of white paste to a 6cm (2⅜in) sausage for the body. Bend in the middle, and then bend one end again to make a 'Z' shape. The smaller end will become the head.

3 Pinch down the sides of the head to form the muzzle, and gently shape the head to form a forehead. Dampen the top of the front legs and press the chest on to the tops of the legs.

4 Roll out tan paste thinly and cut out two 2cm (¾in) ovals. Dampen and stick on either side of the face as shown. Mark the eyes and nose with a Dresden tool and insert edible black sugar pearls.

5 Make a tiny short pointed cone of white paste for the tail and stick it on.

6 Make a tiny pink flattened cone for the tongue. Attach it so that it sticks out as shown. Make another small cone of white paste for the bottom jaw, and stick that in place under the tongue.

7 Roll out the black and tan paste thinly. Cut two 3cm (1¼in) ovals of tan for the ears and small irregular shapes of both colours to stick on to the body.

8 Stick the ears to the sides of the head, hanging straight down.

9 Make two tiny sausages of paste for the eyebrows. Stick above the eyes.

10 Shape two 3g (¹⁄₁₀oz) pieces of white paste to 3cm (1¼in) carrot shapes for back legs; flatten the fat end of each and curve it towards the paw. Dampen and stick to the sides of the back end of the body, toes facing forwards.

Dalmatian

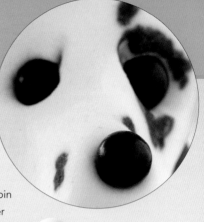

Materials:

30g (1oz) brown modelling paste

25g (just under 1oz) white modelling paste

Small amount of red modelling paste

Edible candy sticks

Edible black sugar pearls

Black food colour pen

Tools:

Dresden tool

Water brush

Thin palette knife

Cutting wheel

Small non-stick rolling pin

Small petal shape cutter

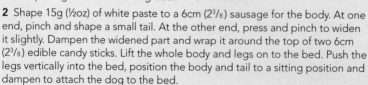

Instructions:

1 Shape 20g (²/₃oz) of brown modelling paste to a 6 x 4cm (2³/₈ x 1½in) oval for the bed. Make a long sausage with 10g (¹/₃oz) of brown paste. Measure the length by wrapping around the bed edge (it is around 16cm (6¼in). Flatten slightly with a rolling pin. If necessary, cut along the length to neaten the edge. Cut both ends neatly, dampen and wrap around the bed, leaving a small opening to look like a dog bed.

2 Shape 15g (½oz) of white paste to a 6cm (2³/₈) sausage for the body. At one end, pinch and shape a small tail. At the other end, press and pinch to widen it slightly. Dampen the widened part and wrap it around the top of two 6cm (2³/₈) edible candy sticks. Lift the whole body and legs on to the bed. Push the legs vertically into the bed, position the body and tail to a sitting position and dampen to attach the dog to the bed.

3 For each back leg, make a 4cm (1½in) carrot using 2.5g (¹/₁₀oz) of white paste. Press the fat end to widen it. Bend it in the middle. Mark the toes with a knife. Dampen and attach to the base of the body.

4 Roll out red modelling paste thinly to make the bandana. Cut a 4cm (1½in) square, then cut diagonally to make a triangle. Dampen and wrap around the top of the body. Pinch together at the back of the neck.

5 Make a 5g (⅙oz) long pear shape of white paste for the head. Gently pinch down the sides of the narrow end to form the muzzle. Mark indentations for the eyes and nose using the Dresden tool and insert edible black sugar pearls. Make a tiny cone for the bottom jaw and

stick it in with the rounded end under the nose. Dampen the top of the neck and push the head gently into place. Allow to dry for a couple of hours.

6 Roll out white paste thinly. Cut out two small petal shapes for ears. Attach to the back of the head, points upwards, then fold the tips forward.

7 Use the black edible food colour pen to draw random-shaped dots all over the dog. This job is much easier if the surface of the paste is fully dry.

King Charles Spaniel

Materials:

30g (1oz) purple modelling paste

25g (just under 1oz) white modelling paste

10g (¹/₃oz) white sugarpaste

Edible candy sticks

Edible black sugar pearls

Brown edible powder food colour

Food grade alcohol for painting

Tools:

Dresden tool

Fine paintbrush

Water brush

Thin palette knife

Cutting wheel

Small non-stick
    rolling pin

Small oval shape cutter

Plastic food bag/
    airtight box

Instructions:

1 Use all the purple modelling paste to shape a 4cm (1½in) square pillow. Pinch the corners.

2 Shape 10g (¹/₃oz) of white paste to a 4cm (1½in) sausage. At one end pinch and shape a small tail and mark it with the Dresden tool to suggest fur. At the other end, press and pinch to widen it slightly. Dampen the widened part and wrap it around the top of two 4cm (1½in) edible candy sticks. Lift the whole body and legs on to the cushion. Push the legs vertically into the cushion, shape the body and tail into a sitting position, dampen and attach the dog to the pillow.

3 Shape 5g (¹/₆oz) of white paste to a short pear shape. Turn up the narrow end slightly for the nose. Shape the fat end gently to form a higher forehead. Mark the eyes and nose with a Dresden tool and insert edible black sugar pearls. Make a tiny cone for the bottom jaw and stick it in with the rounded end under the nose. Dampen the top of the neck and press the head into place. For best results leave the dog to dry overnight before adding the fur.

4 Shape lots of tiny 1–2cm (³⁄₈–¾in) sausages from white sugarpaste and keep them in a plastic food bag or airtight box to keep them soft. Dampen the front legs; attach two or three of the tiny sausages of paste at a time, starting at the paws, with the paste draping over the pillow. Use the Dresden tool or knife to mark long fur, thinning it over the pillow. Continue up the legs, overlapping the paste, to create long fur up to the neck, covering the candy sticks.

5 For the body fur, use 5g (¹⁄₆oz) of white sugarpaste to make a sausage approximately 4cm (1½in) long. Flatten and widen it and try it for size over the body; it should be slightly wider, so that the fur hides all the smooth paste on the body. Use the Dresden tool to mark lots of lines to make long fur, making the edges look feathered. Dampen the back and drape the fur over, blending in where it touches the cushion.

6 Roll out white modelling paste thinly and cut out two small ovals for ears. Mark the fur using the Dresden tool. Dampen and attach to the sides of the head.

7 Paint brown parts using brown powder food colour mixed with alcohol.

Sheepdog

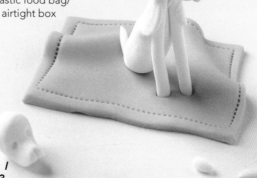

Materials:

30g (1oz) pink modelling paste

25g (just under 1oz) white modelling paste

20g (²/₃oz) white sugarpaste

Small amount of grey sugarpaste

Edible candy sticks

Edible black sugar pearls

Tools:

Dresden tool

Water brush

Thin palette knife

Cutting wheel

Stitching wheel

Small non-stick rolling pin

Plastic food bag/ airtight box

Instructions:

1 Roll out pink modelling paste thickly. Cut a blanket approximately 8 x 6cm (3¹/₈ x 2³/₈in). Mark with the stitching wheel.

2 Shape 15g (½oz) white modelling paste to a 6cm (2³/₈in) sausage for the body. At one end, pinch and shape a small tail. At the other end, press and pinch to widen it slightly. Dampen the widened part and wrap it around the top of two 6cm (2³/₈in) edible candy sticks. Lift the whole body and legs on to the blanket. Push the legs vertically into the blanket, place the body and tail in a sitting position and dampen to attach the dog.

3 Make a 5g (¹/₆oz) long pear shape of white modelling paste for the head. Gently pinch down the sides of the narrow end to form the muzzle. Mark indentations for the eyes and nose using the Dresden tool and insert edible black sugar pearls.

4 Make a tiny cone of pink modelling paste for the tongue, flatten it slightly, dampen and attach it so it hangs out of the mouth. Make a tiny cone of white paste for the bottom jaw and stick it in with the rounded end under the nose. Dampen the top of the neck and push the head gently into place. Allow to dry for a couple of hours or overnight.

5 Shape lots of tiny 1–2cm (³/₈–¾in) sausages of white sugarpaste and a few grey ones for fur. Keep them in a plastic food bag or airtight box to keep them soft. Dampen the candy stick legs and attach two or three tiny sausages at a time, starting at the paws and draping over the blanket. Use the Dresden tool or knife to mark long fur, thinning it where it lies over the blanket. Continue up the legs, overlapping the paste, and making it look like long fur up to the neck. The fur should cover the candy sticks. Dampen the tail and add more long fur to drape over the blanket. Continue up the body, making patches of grey and blending in each time. On the head, start in the middle of the head and nose, so that the fur hangs down.

6 Stick a few strands together and attach to the sides of the head, pointing upwards, and then let the fur bend down sideways. Add more strands where needed.

Poodle

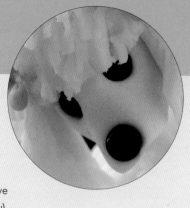

Materials:

30g (1oz) pink modelling paste

Edible sugar candy sticks

15g (½oz) white modelling paste

Very small amount of white sugarpaste

Edible black sugar pearls

Clear piping gel (optional)

Tools:

Stitching wheel

Dresden tool

Water brush

Thin palette knife

Tea strainer/small sieve

Multi-mould (tiny bow)

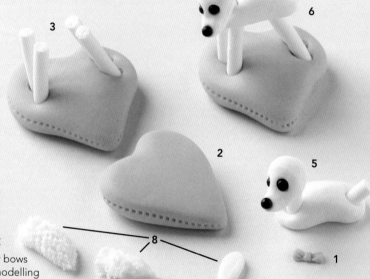

Instructions:

1 Make two tiny bows using the pink modelling paste in the tiny bow mould.

2 Use the rest of the pink modelling paste to shape a 4cm (1½in) heart cushion. Mark round the edge with the stitching wheel.

3 Push in two 3cm (1¼in) candy sticks at the angle shown, then two in vertically, for the legs. Make sure that the tops of the sticks have only 3cm (1¼in) between the front and back pairs to allow space for the body. Trim the tops of the vertical legs to be level with the tops of the back legs.

4 Shape 5g (¹/₆oz) of white modelling paste to a 3cm (1¼in) sausage for the body. Push in a short edible candy stick vertically for the neck, and a shorter piece at an angle for the tail.

5 Shape 2.5g (¹/₁₀oz) white modelling paste to a long pear shape for the head. Turn up the narrow end slightly for the nose. Pinch and shape the sides of the muzzle to make them hang down more. Shape the fat end of the head gently to form a higher forehead. Mark the eyes and nose with a Dresden tool and insert edible black sugar pearls. Dampen the top of the neck and press the head into place.

6 Dampen the tops of the legs and push the body into place, head end above the vertical legs. Leave to dry overnight.

7 Dampen the areas where the fluff will go. Push white sugarpaste through the tea strainer or sieve to make fluff. When you have the length you want, cut it off with a knife and attach it to the dampened areas on the dog. Press into place with a Dresden tool; don't press with fingers as you may flatten the fluff. If you have trouble getting it to stay on, use clear piping gel as a glue instead of dampening with water.

8 For the ears, make two small ovals. Dampen the sides of the head and attach them, hanging down. Dampen the ears and cut and attach some fluff. Attach the tiny pink bows at the tops of the ears.

St Bernard

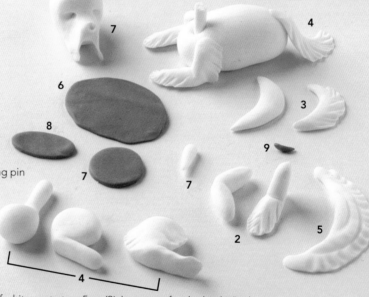

Materials:

70g (2½oz) white modelling paste
20g (²⁄₃oz) tan modelling paste
Edible candy stick
Edible black sugar pearls
Black food colour pen

Tools:

Small oval cutter
Small circle cutter
Dresden tool
Dusting brush
Water brush
Thin palette knife
Plastic food bag/
    airtight box
Small non-stick rolling pin

Instructions:

1 Shape 30g (1oz) of white paste to a 5cm (2in) sausage for the body. Push in short candy stick vertically for the neck.

2 Make a 4cm (1½in) sausage from 2.5g (¹⁄₁₀oz) of white paste for each front leg. Bend in half to form a right angle. Mark over the edges with a Dresden tool to look like long fur. Mark toes with a knife. Attach the legs to the side of the body with the paws pointing forwards and use the Dresden tool to blend in the fur to the body.

3 Shape 2g (¹⁄₁₂oz) of paste to a 4cm (1½in) long cone shape for the tail. Press down one edge, then mark long fur with the Dresden tool. Attach to the body.

4 For each back leg, shape a 5g (¹⁄₆oz) ball of white paste and roll one end to 4cm (1½in) long. Flatten the wide end slightly and bend at right angles in the middle. Mark fur with the Dresden tool as before. Mark toes with a knife. Stick the legs to the sides of the body, paws pointing forwards.

5 Shape an 8cm (3¹⁄₈in) sausage from 5g (¹⁄₆oz) white paste for the chest fur. Flatten slightly and mark folds of skin and fur using the Dresden tool. Attach to the front of the chest, joining behind the neck.

6 Roll out the tan paste thinly. Cut an oval shape roughly the size of the dog's back. Dampen and lay it on the back. Texture and blend in the edges with the Dresden tool.

7 Make a long pear shape from 15g (½oz) white paste for the head. Pinch and shape the sides of the muzzle and forehead. Roll out the tan paste thinly. Cut out and stick on two small circles for the colour on the dog's face, and two ovals for his ears (keep covered until the head

is on the body). Mark the eyes and nose with a Dresden tool and insert edible black sugar pearls. Make a tiny cone of white paste for the bottom jaw and stick it on with the rounded end under the nose. Dampen the top of the neck and press the head into place.

8 Cut out ovals of tan paste for the ears. Attach the long front edges to the sides of the face.

9 Make two tiny sausages of tan paste, curve slightly, and stick on over the eyes.

Border Collie

Materials:

25g (just under 1oz) white modelling paste

10g (1/3oz) black modelling paste

Edible candy sticks

Edible black sugar pearls

Tools

Dresden tool

Water brush

Thin palette knife

Cutting wheel

Small non-stick rolling pin

Small oval cutter

Small petal cutter

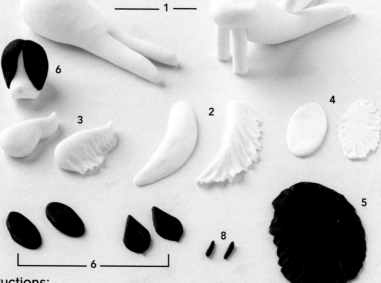

Instructions:

1 Shape 15g (½oz) of white paste into a 7cm (2¾in) long carrot for the body. Cut 3cm (1¼in) lengthways into the narrow end. Turn the cut edges down to the work surface. Mark toes with a knife. Push in a short candy stick at the top of the legs to support the head. Raise the back end of the body and push two 2.5cm (1in) edible candy sticks into the underside, as shown. Leave to dry for a couple of hours or overnight.

2 Shape 2g (1/12oz) of paste to a 4cm (1½in) long cone shape for the tail. Press down one edge, then mark long fur with the Dresden tool. Attach to the body.

3 Shape 2g (1/12oz) of white paste to a 2.5cm (1in) long cone for each back leg. Flatten the wide end slightly and bend at right angles in the middle. Mark fur with the Dresden tool. Mark toes with a knife. Stick the legs to the sides of the body, hiding the candy stick supports, paws pointing forwards.

4 Roll out the white paste thinly. Cut a small oval for the chest fur. Texture the edges with the Dresden tool. Dampen and lay it in front of the neck, over the front legs.

5 Roll out the black paste thinly. Cut an oval shape (does not have to be perfect) roughly the size of the dog's back. Dampen and lay it on the back. Texture and blend in the edges with the Dresden tool.

6 Make a 5g (1/6oz) long pear shape of white paste for the head. Gently pinch down the sides of the narrow end to form the muzzle. Mark indentations for the eyes and nose using the Dresden tool. Roll out the black paste thinly and cut out and stick on two small ovals for the patches on the face. Also cut out two small petals for the ears and keep them covered until the head is on the body. Insert edible black sugar pearls for the eyes and nose. Make a tiny cone for the bottom jaw and stick it on with the rounded end under the nose. Dampen the top of the neck and push the head gently into place.

7 Attach the ears to the back of the head, points upwards, then fold the tips forward.

8 Make two tiny sausages of black paste, curve slightly, and stick on over the eyes.

Shitzu

Materials:

20g (²/₃oz) pale cream modelling paste

10g (¹/₃oz) pale cream sugarpaste

Edible candy stick

Edible black sugar pearls

Grey and dark brown edible powder food colour

Tools:

Small petal cutter

Dresden tool

Dusting brush

Water brush

Thin palette knife

Tea strainer/small sieve

Plastic food bag/ airtight box

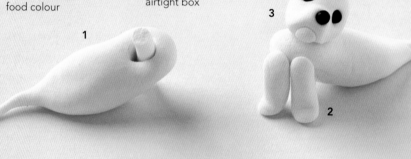

Instructions:

1 Shape 10g (¹/₃oz) of modelling paste to a 4cm (1½in) sausage for the body. Pinch and shape one end to form a short pointed tail. Dampen a 3cm (1¼in) edible candy stick in the middle and push right through to form a neck support and to raise the body.

2 Make two 2cm (¾in) long sausages for the front legs and stick them in place.

3 Shape 5g (¹/₆oz) of modelling paste to a short pear shape for the head. Turn up the narrow end slightly for the nose. Shape the fat end gently to form a higher forehead. Mark the eyes and nose with a Dresden tool and insert edible black sugar pearls. Make a tiny cone for the bottom jaw and stick it in with the rounded end under the nose. Dampen the top of the neck and press the head into place, tilting backwards to look cute. Texture the tail with the Dresden tool. For best results leave the dog to dry overnight before adding more fur.

4 Make a small amount of fluff by pushing sugarpaste through the tea strainer or sieve. Dampen the chin and attach the fluff.

5 Shape lots of tiny 1–2cm (³/₈–¾in) sausages of sugarpaste for fur and keep them under plastic so they stay soft. Dampen the front legs; attach two or three of the tiny sausages of paste at a time, starting at the paws, draping over the work surface. Use the Dresden tool or knife to mark long fur, thinning it where it lies over the work surface. Continue up the legs, overlapping the paste, to create long fur up to the neck, hiding the candy sticks. Dampen the tail and add more long fur. Continue up the body, adding more strands, blending in each time. On the head, start in the middle of the head and nose, so that the fur hangs down. Make sure that the eyes and nose can be seen.

6 Shape two small pea-sized pieces of modelling paste to 1cm (³/₈in) teardrops for the ears. Mark lines for the fur. Attach to the side of the head. Add another couple of strands of thin fur.

7 Brush grey and dark brown edible powder food colour on the edges of the ears, round the mouth and over the back.

Snow Dog Puppy

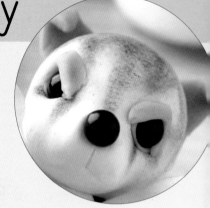

Materials:

30g (1oz) blue modelling paste

25g (just under 1oz) white modelling paste

Grey edible powder food colour

Edible candy stick

Edible black sugar pearls

Pale pink edible food colour pen

Tools:

Small petal cutter

Dresden tool

Dusting brush

Water brush

Thin palette knife

Small petal shape cutter

Small non-stick rolling pin

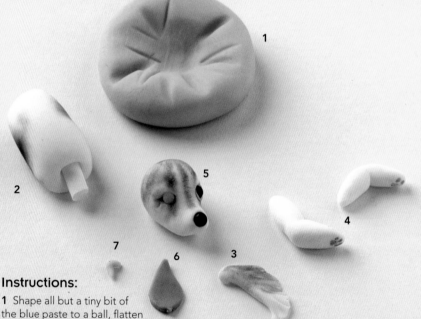

Instructions:

1 Shape all but a tiny bit of the blue paste to a ball, flatten slightly, then push the middle in to make a dip for the puppy to lie in. Mark creases using the Dresden tool.

2 Shape 20g (²/₃oz) of white paste to a 3cm (1¼in) sausage for the body. Push in a short edible candy stick as a support for the head. Brush with grey powder food colour over the back, leaving the tummy white. Lay the body in the bed and dampen underneath to stick.

3 Shape 1g (¹/₂₄oz) of white paste to a 2cm (¾in) long cone shape for the tail. Press down one edge, then mark long fur with the Dresden tool. Brush with grey edible powder food colour and attach to the body.

4 Cut a 5g (¹/₆oz) piece of white paste into four equal pieces for the legs. Roll to form 3cm (1¼in) sausages. Bend to form 'L' shapes and attach two as front legs to the top of the body, paws pointing away from the head.

Attach the back legs to the sides of the body at the tail end, paws pointing to the head. Draw pads on the base of the paws using the pink edible food colour pen.

5 Shape 5g (^{1}/$_6$oz) of white paste to a short pear shape for the head. Turn up the narrow end slightly for the nose. Shape the fat end gently to form a higher forehead. Mark the eyes and nose with a Dresden tool. Roll tiny balls of blue paste, flatten, dampen and stick in the eye sockets. Insert edible black sugar pearls for the nose and eyeballs. Make a tiny cone for the bottom jaw and stick it on with the rounded end under the nose. Dampen the top of the neck and press the head into place. Brush the head with grey edible powder food colour.

6 Roll out white paste thinly. Cut out two small petals. Attach to the back of the head, points upwards, then fold the tips forward. Brush with grey edible powder food colour.

7 Make two tiny sausages of white paste, curve slightly, brush with grey edible powder food colour and stick on over the eyes.

Acknowledgements
My thanks to all at Search Press and to Paul Bricknell for the photography.

You are invited to visit the author's website: www.franklysweet.co.uk for more information and video tutorials.

Publisher's Note
If you would like more information about sugarcraft, try the following books by the same author, all published by Search Press:
Twenty to Make Sugar Animals
Twenty to Make Sugar Birds
Twenty to Make Sugar Fairies
Sensational Sugar Animals
Twenty to Make Mini Sugar Shoes
Twenty to Make Mini Sugar Bags
Sensational Sugar Fairies